This book
belongs to:

Jose Carlos Rodriquez

_____

Marietta Reads!
because
Kiwanis Club of Marietta
cares.

Marietta Reads!
We All Succeed When Marietta Reads

The Journey of Sir Douglas Fir

A Reader's Musical

Story by Bill Barnes • Written by Ric Reitz • Illustrations by David Brewer
Music & Original Score by Jim Ellis • Lyrics by Ric Reitz

Sir Fir Books

Atlanta / Toronto

THE JOURNEY OF
SIR DOUGLAS FIR

A Reader's Musical

Story by Bill Barnes • Written by Ric Reitz • Illustrations by David Brewer
Music & Original Score by Jim Ellis • Lyrics by Ric Reitz

Sir Fir Books & Music
c/o Sir Fir Enterprises, LLC
1468 Shadowrock Heights • Marietta, Georgia 30062, U.S.A.
Toll Free (877) 565-7020 • sirdouglasfir.com

For more information about The GRAMMY® Foundation's Leonard Bernstein Center for Learning® contact:

The GRAMMY Foundation
3402 Pico Boulevard • Santa Monica, CA 90405
www.grammy.com

Published in Canada by Sir Fir Books, August 1999 • Published in U.S.A., November 1999
Copyright ©℗1999 Sir Fir Enterprises, LLC • All rights reserved. • Sir Douglas Fir is a registered trademark of Sir Fir Enterprises, LLC.
Library of Congress Catalog Card Number: 99-93709 • ISBN 0-9670160-0-2
Printed in U.S.A. • Second Printing, November 2000

To everyone who courageously faces change
and somehow finds a rainbow.

Read & Sing Along Produced by Ric Reitz
Recorded at: Crunch Sound, Toronto, Ontario and Doppler Studios, Atlanta, Georgia
Engineered and Edited by Granger Beam at Doppler Studios, Atlanta, Georgia
Songs and Score Produced by Jim Ellis

Story Edited by Suzanne Bell
Book Design by Paula Chance and Wendy Harrison-Severin
CD Design by Paula Chance

AUDIO THEATER CAST

Narrator	Bob Gillies
Sir Douglas Fir	Jeff Winter
Sir Douglas Fir (Vocals)	Mike Gleason
Earl Squirrel	Johnny Cenicola
Monk the Skunk	Bruce Dow
Rona Redbreast	Barbara Mantini
Bully Bear	George Masswohl
Cedric the Otter	Shawn Wright
Mrs. O'Deer	Valerie Boyle
Queen's Rep	Valerie Boyle
Ranger	Michael Lamport
Conductor	Michael Lamport
Mill Boss	Jack Duffy
Young Fir	Susan Bennett
Young Fir (Vocals)	Jennifer Griffin
Young Oak	Scott Hilley
Young Oak (Vocals)	John McGrath

The word "overture" can mean many things.   In this case, it is an introduction to
a piece of musical work. It may seem out of place   in a book, but not when you
consider that this Read & Sing Along version of   *The Journey of Sir Douglas Fir*
is actually a mini-musical presented in book   form.

The CD that accompanies this book begins with an overture.
May this overture be the beginning of a unique reading
adventure that will inspire young people for a lifetime.

[To read the story without the CD, the option exists
to simply skip the songs.]

CHAPTER ONE

SHAWNIGAN LAKE

Somewhere between "once upon a time" and "happily ever after," it was the beginning of summer in a magical forest near Shawnigan Lake, British Columbia. And summertime at Shawnigan Lake was always the best time. Instead of chilly days or freezing Canadian nights, a soft warm breeze blew in from the Pacific Ocean and through the lush green valleys of Vancouver Island to bid all the forest creatures "good morning," and that made everybody happy, everybody except Douglas Fir.

Normally, the ever cheerful Douglas was first to smile when summer's trade winds gently tickled his exposed roots, the bark on his mammoth 200-foot (60.96m) body, and the tips of his wispy green needles. But not this day, though he couldn't quite figure out why. Perhaps he was feeling odd because he had just celebrated his 350th birthday, which automatically made summers seem shorter and winters feel that much longer. Or, was he simply tired of the same old routine?

Shawnigan Lake Song

A change in the wind.
A change in the season.
I'm not feeling right.
Don't know the reason.

I like where I am,
   the forest floor chatter,
   the beautiful sights,
   but something's the matter.

I can't say what it might be.
I can't tell if it's just me.
'Cause life's always the same.
Life's always the same.
Can I fully know this game
   when life's always the same
   at Shawnigan Lake?

A typical day shift
   at Shawnigan Lake
   begins before sunrise
   and never past eight.

All of the insects
   in Shawnigan Glen
   exercise daily
   exactly at ten.

The worker bees,
   as they hum a tune,
   pollinate flowers
   precisely at noon.

We're never short
   of things to do,
   'cause we start over
   at 3:02 . . .

For so many years
   I've witnessed the clockwork
   tick my life away.
It's making my rings hurt.

What I wouldn't give
   to alter that beat,
   or once make the sun
   set down in the East.

I can't say what it might be.
I can't tell if it's just me.
'Cause life's always the same.
Life's always the same.
Can I fully know this game
   when life's always the same
   at Shawnigan Lake?

I'm old for a human;
   not old for a tree.
Can hope make a diff'rence
   to someone like me?

I wonder each day
   what's over the ridge.
Could I get a peak
   at one little smidge?!

Oh, he can't say what it
   might be.
Who can see (who can see)
   their destiny?
His life's always the same.
No one is to blame.
Can I fully know this game
   when life's always the same
   at Shawnigan Lake?!

While Douglas's thoughts drifted, little Earl Squirrel came running up a path
with hardly enough breath to blow out a candle on a birthday cake, had
it been his birthday and had there been a cake.

"Twiglets! It's Twiglet Day!"

Bringing his thoughts back to his world, Douglas warmly responded, "Indeed.
It's Twiglet Day. And right on schedule." Then, Douglas noticed a park ranger
pushing a wheelbarrow toward him. In the wheelbarrow were two twiglets.

All the forest creatures know that a twiglet is a baby tree. Raised in a
tree nursery, a twiglet grows up to go to school like anyone else.
Twiglets go to Pre-Tree School, where they learn all they
need to know about being an adult tree.

Douglas was the most respected and popular teacher around, and Twiglet Day was one of several days each year the friendly park ranger brought all the twiglets who had studied hard to Douglas for their final test.

Earl, who had a habit of getting into everybody's business whether he was welcome or not, climbed onto the ranger's wheelbarrow to face the twiglets. "I want to be a tree and take the test with you!"

"You can't be in our class. You can't be a squirrel and a tree, too!"

"Haven't you ever heard of a tree squirrel?" Earl cracked, cackling at his own joke as he fell off the ranger's wheelbarrow.

The twiglets were not amused, especially when Douglas began the test and Earl tried to answer all the questions.

"Do you know what kind of trees you are?"

Earl spoke first. "One's an oak tree; one's a fir tree! One has leaves; one has needles . . ."

The twiglets fought back, "Douglas, this isn't fair!"

Although the mighty fir had a special place in his heart for Earl, Douglas had to agree. But Earl would not stop.

A B C D E F G H I

Pre-Tree School

"Class? Attention.
  Attention, please!"

What are these?
They're branches!
They hold up all . . . ?
The leaves!
On fir trees . . . ?
The needles!

"The pollen makes me sneeze!"

I stand on . . . ?
My roots!
They're so snug down in the ground.
My coat's made . . . ?
Of bark!
That I wear year 'round.

In autumn all the leaves will drop
   to make way for the winter.
In spring look for the buds to pop.
It couldn't be much simpler.
Simpler!

The rain helps me . . . ?
Grow tall!
Puts me right in the mood.
The sun takes . . . ?
The water!
Turns it to food.

I share my shade most happily.
There's nothing that I'd rather be.
I'm a tree!
I'm a tree!
I'm a tree!
I'm a tree!
Earl, you'll never be a tree!

INK
FOREST GRE

When the class was finally over, Douglas gave Earl a stern look, then motioned to the ranger. "You can give them their diplomas. In spite of Earl, I can see they did their homework."

"Sure thing, Douglas. I'll go plant them now. And take care, a big storm's coming."

As the ranger took the twiglets away, Earl could sense that Douglas was not pleased with him and tried to sneak off. But Douglas quickly stopped Earl in his tracks. "Wait a minute, young man! The next time I'm teaching and you answer *all* the questions, I'll . . . I'll . . ."

"What?" chirped a voice from out of nowhere.
"You'll what?"

Diploma

Phi

Beta

Sappa

Douglas Fir

Teacher

Douglas looked up to see who had interrupted him. Of course, he already knew it was Rona Redbreast, the local gossip bird and editor of *The Daily Forest* newspaper.

"Well?" Rona persisted. "I'm waiting."

"Oh, you distracted me, and I've lost my thought."

"Ah-ha! Where did you leave it? I'm an expert at finding lost things. It's part of being a good reporter."

Rona began to look high and low. She looked behind branches and under rocks, then finally settled next to a mysterious pile of leaves that rustled a bit.

"I found it! Come out, lost thought!"

The pile moved again.

Earl cautiously interrupted. "How will we know if that's a lost thought? Have you ever seen one? Are they like monsters? What if they're big and hairy?"

Rona stopped short. She hadn't thought of that. "Douglas, you look down on that pile."

But before Douglas could wake up his lost thought, the pile jumped and a thing popped out.

Rona was so frightened she fell over backwards and knocked her head on the ground.

"Can't a guy get a little sleep around here?" the thing snorted, as it brushed leaves off its black and white stripes. It was their lazy friend, Monk the Skunk.

Douglas sighed. "Oh, it's just you, Monk. Earl, would you help Madame Redbreast?"

Earl ran down to the lake, dipped an acorn cap in the cool water, and dashed back up the hill to splash it on Rona.

When Rona sat up she noticed everyone staring at her and became very embarrassed. "Well, I knew it was Monk all along. Everyone knows a lost thought never hides under leaves. But I'll still find it!"

"I'm sure you will," Douglas assured her, before changing the subject. "What big news stories are you covering today?"

"Well, if you must know, I'm writing a story about the summer tourist season, which officially begins today."

"Oh, that's right! I'd forgotten that, too!" Douglas cried out, which made Rona feel better since she had helped him remember something.

Of course, the tourist talk got Monk's attention quick. "You mean free food?" He loved food, free or otherwise, as did Rona. So they quickly scampered away, leaving a suddenly sorrowful Earl behind with Douglas.

NATURE TRAIL

CAMP SITES

"What's wrong, Earl? You love summertime and the tourists as much as everyone else."

"Yeah, but I was just thinking about what happens at the end of this summer. Kindergarten."

"You're not afraid of school are you? You always do well in my classes. Too well, in fact."

Earl kicked at the ground. "I love being in your class. I'm just afraid that everyone will forget me when I'm gone."

"Earl, you don't have to be with me to live in my thoughts."

"But you just lost a thought."

"Oh . . ." Douglas realized that Earl was deeply troubled. "But I *never* forget friends like you."

When Douglas noticed a look of surprise on Earl's face, he continued. "Be thankful you have the chance to try new things. I'd like to do something a little different."

Momentarily distracted by a distant thunderclap, Earl was confused. "You don't like being a tree?"

"Oh, sure I do. It's just that new experiences make me feel more *alive*. They make me a better teacher and friend. I dream about new adventures all the time."

"Don't new things scare you?"

"Sometimes. But, here's a deal. I'll help you get ready for kindergarten, if you promise to help me someday."

"What could I ever do for you? I'm only a little squirrel."

"You help me a lot just by being my friend."

"Even while I'm away?"

Douglas nodded. And Earl squealed his approval.

Yes, even though things seemed to stay the same for Douglas, he had to admit that life at Shawnigan Lake had its rewards.

Joined at the Dreams

"Are we *best* friends?"

"My mother once told me that friends
become *best* friends the moment
they share their dreams."

"Really?"

"Really."

When someone shares a dream with you,
when spirits share a point of view,
two paths converge to start one new,
a soul's revealed, a bond is sealed.

A friendship starts on faith alone;
a hope, a prayer, you're almost home.
But forever friendships aren't full grown
until you see that part of me . . .

that wishes upon a star ev'ry night,
that soars on the tail of a moonbeam's light,
that slays all the dragons that hide out of sight,
that fills me with delight.

Once you reveal the secrets within,
you won't walk alone, won't be scared to begin.
And being apart's not as hard as it seems
when we're joined at the dreams.

"Do you think we could share
some dreams?"

"I think so. You go first."

"I'd like to grow up to be just like you,
big and strong. And you're always
nice to everyone. And I'd like to be
a teacher."

"Teachers have to go to school."

"Oh, yeah."

"It's not so bad."

"What about your dreams?"

"Well, I've always lived here, and I love
it. But just once I'd like to visit other
places and try something new."

"Maybe I could help."

"And I'll help you."

"And we'll be *best* friends, right?"

"Right."

Because you've seen that part of me . . .
that wishes upon a star ev'ry night,
that soars on the tail of a moonbeam's light,
that slays all the dragons that hide out of sight,
that fills me with delight.

Once we reveal the secrets within,
we won't walk alone, won't be scared to begin.
And being apart's not as hard as it seems
when we're joined at the dreams.

"Feel better?"

"Can I go play with the others?"

"Sure."

CHAPTER TWO

THE STORM

The rumble of nearby thunder caused the earth to shake below Douglas. He remembered the ranger's warning that a storm was coming, and now it was nearly upon him. The air had an eerie smell, and Douglas sensed this storm would be one of the bad ones. He braced himself against the swirling wind and warned the other trees and animals. "Take cover! Pass on the news!"

One by one the trees yelled, and their warnings echoed long and loud through the woods. Then the storm hit.

The wind whipped at Douglas's limbs, nearly pulling the needles off, and the rain slapped against his bark so hard that it hurt. He dug his roots deeper into the ground to have a better chance of staying upright.

Of all the terrors of a storm, lightning was the most frightening to Douglas; it could strike in the forest and cause a tree to split or FALL.

Suddenly, Douglas began to lean. And when his roots started to pop out of the ground he screamed, "Help! Help!"

The rain-soaked earth made a desperate attempt to hold on, as Douglas shuddered and shook. His tall trunk bowed and rocked with each new gust of wind.

Earl and Monk came running as soon as they heard their friend was in trouble. They jumped up and down on Douglas's roots to stuff them back into the ground, but it was no use. Douglas was too big. He weighed too much.

BOOM! BOOM! More lightning and thunder roared through the forest.

Then, with a loud CRASH, all 200 feet (60.96m) of Douglas fell to the ground. And Earl shrieked, "Douglas, don't leave me!"

The storm lasted all night and slipped away with the morning light. The sun, which must be afraid of storms, too, because it's never around when there is one, peeked over the mountains to look at the damage.

Earl, Monk, and a few other friends — Mrs. O'Deer, Bully Bear, and a very intelligent otter, Cedrick — all inched out of their hiding places to check on Douglas.

Earl was the bravest and approached Douglas first. Well, actually, Bully Bear pushed him over to Douglas, but no one else saw it.

Mrs. O'Deer did what she did best — she cried, "Oh dear, oh dear."

And, after a few moments, Douglas moaned.

"He's alive!" shouted a jubilant Earl, ever thankful that his friend hadn't left him.

Douglas struggled to speak. "Lift me up, everybody. Push up on my branches so I can put my 'toes' back into the dirt."

All the animals got behind a big branch and pushed,
and pushed, but nothing happened.

Just then, a thought occurred to Cedrick. "Maybe if
we push up on a smaller branch he'll be lighter?"

That made sense. So they all pushed up
on a smaller branch, but that
didn't work either.

It was time
to consult
the ranger.

When the ranger arrived, he just shook his head. "I'm sorry, Douglas. You can't be what you used to be. We can't put a tree as big as you are back in the ground."

Mrs. O'Deer sobbed, "Oh dear!"

Cedrick interrupted, "Wait! I read that when trees can't be trees, they lose all their leaves, or needles in this case, and can become useful to man."

Everyone gasped, except the ranger, of course.

Bully Bear had heard enough. He stomped over to the ranger and threatened to bite his knee. "If Douglas wants to stay a tree, I say he stays a tree!"

Douglas motioned for Bully to stop. "No, Bully. I wanted change, and I *got* it. Though I never imagined *this*. It can't be undone. I guess it's time for me to be something else. I just don't know what."

Nobody seemed to know. But the thought of helping Douglas decide got everybody excited. Whose idea would he accept? There would be a contest!

THE CONTEST

The news spread far and wide that the contest was to be the greatest contest in the history of Shawnigan Lake. True, it was the *only* contest in the history of Shawnigan Lake, but nobody bothered to mention that and spoil the fun.

Rona stood on Douglas's trunk and tried to get everyone's attention. "Excuse me! Excuse me, please!" But nobody was listening. So, at the top of her lungs, she screamed, "QUIET!" until everyone settled down.

"Remember, it doesn't matter who wins the contest; it only matters that Douglas approves of his new destiny . . . and that there are prizes." Everyone agreed with that.

"The grand prize winner will be allowed to accompany Douglas on his journey, wherever it may take him. Who wants to go first?"

As you can well imagine, everyone's hand went up at once.

It was quickly decided that Bully Bear would go first because he made the meanest face. He wanted Douglas to be a pirate ship, but no one else liked that idea.

I see him sailing oceans blue,
commanding a great crew,
knowing what to do.
With pirates, he'll rule while he's afloat.
I think he should be . . .
I think he should be a boat!

Monk the Skunk and his brothers went next and wanted Douglas to be a bench seat in a church. They called it a "pew," which is what everyone else thought of their idea.

The Contest Song

Please, let's stop all the noise.
Little girls and boys
    don't require an ocean view.
They need a place to sit,
    need the perfect fit
    of a sturdy wooden pew.

Strong and new,
    wooden pew.
Wouldn't you?
We win.

The contest went on and on. Some wanted Douglas to be a chair; others wanted him to be a desk and a door and a house and just about anything else that could be made out of wood.

Earl waited patiently for his turn. He'd even stayed up late the night before practicing being patient, because he knew he would go last.

Finally, Rona turned to Earl. "You ready?"

"Y-y-yes, I'm ready."

Suddenly, to the horror of all watching, an impatient Bully Bear stood and tore up Earl's speech.

Douglas got very angry. "Bully, Earl will speak!"

At first Earl struggled to find the right words, but eventually he found the strength to say, "Douglas should become a great book of memories, so he can continue being a teacher."

The Contest Song

I think that he should be a great book.
I think you all should know.
I think you should take a good look,
　help generations grow.
He has such memories.
He's lived so long.

"Yeah! He's seen the indians, and
　the settlers, and our families,
　and the tourists, and the . . ."

"Get on with it!"

He belongs!
Douglas is much more than a tree,
　not a pew, not a pirate to me.
We say to you most hum-b-ly . . .
I think he should be . . .
He should be . . .
A book! A book!

Then, Earl nodded respectfully at Douglas and sat down.

Rona didn't have to take a vote. As everyone congratulated Earl, she knew that he was the winner of the contest.

CHAPTER FOUR

AN ADVENTURE

A grand parade was scheduled to send Douglas and Earl off on their trip to a maker of great books in the distant city of Toronto. Unfortunately, the parade had to be canceled. No one knew how to play any instruments except Cedrick. He could play the tuba, but only if some of the others would hold it for him.

Still, everyone gathered to say their good-byes at a nearby train station, because a train was the only way Douglas could travel over land.

"All aboard!" the conductor shouted.

At that moment, many of the animals were afraid for Douglas and Earl: the new place they were going might be strange and scary. Others were sad to think that Douglas was really leaving. But mostly, everyone seemed excited and showed as much courage as they could, even Mrs. O'Deer, who simply said, "Oh dear."

Earl's heart raced. Despite feeling nervous, he pledged to stay with Douglas no matter what might happen, because that's what *best* friends do.

Then, with the toot of the whistle, the train pulled away carrying a long, lean Douglas on three flat cars.

The train rumbled over
the Rocky Mountains,
through the plains of central
Canada, and by sparkling rivers.
Animals kept popping up along
the way, and Earl waved and
whooped — at the antelope and rabbits,
wild horses and cows, and a prairie dog,
who didn't look much like a dog at all,
but Douglas assured Earl he was.

After a while, Earl grew tired of waving and even stopped asking "Are we there yet?," mostly because he was homesick. Douglas admitted that he was too, but reminded himself that one of his lifelong dreams was coming true.

Douglas had always wished he could move around and explore new places, and now, by an act of nature and with the assistance of his friends, he really was. Douglas was suddenly giddy with excitement.

Calgary

Vancouver

Victoria

Are we there yet?

MAIN PORTAGE

Regina
Winnipeg
Thunder Bay
Sault Ste. Marie
TORONTO

The gentle rocking motion of the train and the *clickity-clack* of the wheels on the track were marvelous new sensations.

The train seemed to glide over the rocky terrain. Cool, fresh air lightly brushed through Douglas's needles.

Douglas closed his eyes and imagined that he was flying. Earl squinched his eyes together, too. At that moment life was wonderful, and anything was possible for them.

It's Wonderful

"Let's look on the bright side. So far, this adventure is everything I dreamed it would be. It's wonderful!"

I know for the first time what it's like to fly.
Can you feel the excitement?
Can you imagine that a kid like me could see in a lifetime all the things we've seen?

"Feel better?"

"A little."

"Let's make it a lot."

Rooted to one place I was shut off from the world.
Now my dreams rush before me.

I was so nervous that at first I cried.
Now we can share it with eyes open wide.
'Cause it's wonderful, so wonderful to me.
To we-ee.

"Us."

Yes, it's wonderful, so wonderful to me.
To be free!

"Now you've got the hang of it."

"Yeah, trying to do new things is really fun."

"And you've had the courage all along."

Scared to be somewhere that I've never been,
yet I need that horizon.
I can't believe just how much we've dared.
Please take a picture,
prove that we were here!
'Cause it's wonderful, so wonderful to me.
To we-ee.

"Us!"

Yes, it's wonderful, so wonderful to be free!
Just us three!

"Everybody sing!"

And there's so much more to see!

As Douglas and Earl floated in their fantasy, they didn't notice that someone had joined them in their dreamy game.

Douglas was the first to see the familiar and beaming intruder. "Monk?! You're a stowaway!"

Apparently, Monk had been hiding on the train since it left the station near Shawnigan Lake. He didn't want his friends to go without him.

Of course, the conductor saw Monk, too. "Ay, you with the white stripe! You got to buy a ticket!"

Even if hiding on trains is not a good thing, Douglas and Earl were surely glad to see Monk and bought him the required ticket.

When the train finally rolled to a stop, the sun was setting, and daylight turned to spooky darkness. The conductor announced their arrival. "All off for the wood mill! This is your stop, folks!"

Since there didn't seem to be anyone around to greet them, Earl and Monk hopped off the train and went to look at the mill. After wiping away some dirt on a window, the two peeked inside, and what they saw frightened them.

Earl ran back to warn Douglas; Monk was too startled to run.

By the time Earl and Monk got back to the train, Douglas was gone.

Earl was furious. "They've taken him! We need to find out who's in charge!"

Douglas's little friends were so angry they had to count to ten *twice* just to calm down. They would find out what happened to their noble friend.

CHAPTER FIVE

DESTINY

"What can I do for you boys?" the mill boss asked from somewhere behind a big wooden desk. Earl got right to the point. "We had a contest, and I won!"

"I see."

Monk jumped in. "What my friend is trying to say, Mr. Boss, is that we came all this way to make sure that our friend, Douglas Fir, becomes a great book of memories, and we don't think you make books here!"

The boss thought aloud. "You know, it's very rare when a tree as big and old as Douglas falls down in the woods and isn't splintered or hurt."

Earl took the opportunity to boast. "That's our Douglas."

"Well, with his permission, we're planning to do something quite wonderful, but it's a secret. Do you know what a secret is?"

"Oh, sure, I tell them all the time."

"Good, then you'll know why you've got to wait for the big surprise."

Well, wait and wait they did. For days Monk and Earl waited, and still no sign of Douglas.

Earl's eyes filled with tears. "I can't take it anymore. I promised Douglas I'd help him and I've let him down. How can he face this alone?"

Monk did everything he could to console Earl. "Douglas can take care of himself. And although we'd like to control everything in life, we can't always. We have to believe this will work out."

But Earl wasn't so sure.

Joined at the Dreams Reprise

"I'm not leaving my best friend."

"Okay. Just try to remember what Douglas told
   you about your friendship, and believe in it
   now more than ever."

When someone shares a dream with you,
   when spirits share a point of view,
   no one on earth can split the two,
   no time or space, no distant place.

The seasons change, we face our fear.
We take a chance, new doors appear.
And forever friendships persevere . . .
Because you've seen that part of me . . .

   that wishes upon a star ev'ry night,
   that soars on the tail of a moonbeam's light,
   that slays all the dragons that hide out of sight,
   that fills me with delight.

Once we reveal the secrets within,
   we won't walk alone, won't be scared to begin.
And being apart's not as hard as it seems,
   when we're joined at the dreams.

[Douglas are you there?
Are you hearing my prayer?
I can't see you.
Can you see me here
   from where you are?

Close to me,
   you'll always be
   one who cares.
And being apart's not as hard as it seems,
   when we're joined at the dreams.]

I will be right by your side.

Just then, Monk and Earl heard some music playing not too far away.

Earl instantly perked up. "Listen. What is it?"

"I don't know."

This time, even Monk raced over to where a crowd had gathered to see what the excitement was all about, but the two still couldn't see much of anything.

Earl and Monk climbed to the top of the tallest building they could find and looked out over the crowd. Thousands and thousands of people were gathered at what looked like a huge circus. A big sign told them they were looking down on Exhibition Place.

There in the center of it all was Douglas. He had a broad smile and looked splendid;
he'd had a haircut, was painted all white, and was so shiny.

Monk was nearly breathless. "It's Douglas! He looks different, but he's beautiful."

The mill boss stepped up onto a platform right next to Douglas. "May I have your attention?!
We are very honored that Mr. Douglas Fir has accepted our offer to be the World's Tallest
Wooden Flagpole and hold high our country's biggest flag."

The crowd cheered, while Earl and Monk danced a jig. This was better than they had ever dreamed.
It was perfect for someone as wise and regal as Douglas.

Looking relieved, Monk turned to Earl. "What did I tell ya!
You've got to have faith!"

"Wait, there's more!" the boss continued, turning to a representative of the Queen of England.

"By special order of the queen, I've been asked to dub thee *Sir Douglas Fir*!"

Indeed, Douglas was made a knight, and the queen's friend touched a shiny sword to Douglas's mighty shoulders.

The photographers snapped lots of pictures — so many, in fact, that when everyone closed their eyes they could still see lights flashing.

When the crowd finally left, Earl and Monk stayed to talk to Douglas one last time. "We're very proud of you, *Sir Douglas*."

"Thank you, Monk."

"Are you disappointed you're not a great book of memories?"

"At first I wasn't sure. All of us wanted it so badly. But when they said I could *live on* as a flagpole and have my stories set in bronze, like a book, it was hard to say no. It'll be a great adventure."

Monk nodded, but Earl was unusually silent.

"Don't you want to talk to me, Earl?"

Fighting back some sniffles, Earl eventually spoke. "I wanted to help you."

"You did. You stuck by me the whole time."

"Will we ever see you again, Sir Douglas?"

"You can visit or give me a shout anytime. But we'll have to be apart some, too. Do you think you can do that now?"

"If you can be brave and have a new life, so can I. I'll go to kindergarten."

"Now that's the grownup-sounding Earl I knew was hiding inside. You won't forget me, will you, Earl?"

"I *never* forget friends like you."

"That will give me great comfort and strength."

Then Douglas asked a favor of Earl. "Would you plant a twiglet fir tree in my place back home? It's a big, important job, but I know you can handle it. And maybe, just maybe, when you talk to him, you can pretend you're talking to me."

"I promise."

Finally, it was time to go, so Earl and Monk took turns hugging and kissing Douglas, and they promised to write many letters.

As his dear friends left, Douglas wanted to cry; and he did just a little, but not for long. Summer would be over soon, and Douglas actually looked forward to autumn and winter and spring and the years to come. After all, there were new animals and new people to meet, and there would be plenty of chances for him to teach and recite his memories. He was happy to be the World's Tallest Wooden Flagpole. He was happy to be Sir Douglas Fir!

FOOTNOTE

On August 18, 1977, the World's Tallest Wooden Flagpole was dedicated in a most honorable ceremony, and was christened with the world's largest Canadian flag as thousands of people stood gazing toward the sky, their hearts filled with pride.

The flagpole was presented to the Canadian National Exhibition Association in Toronto by Travel South, U.S.A., and the member states of Alabama, Arkansas, Florida, Georgia, Kentucky, Louisiana, Mississippi, North Carolina, South Carolina, Tennessee, and Virginia, as an expression of appreciation for the visitation of all Canadians to their region and for friendships that have evolved over the years.

The American representative at the dedication was Bill Barnes of Atlanta, Georgia.

At the time this story was made into a book (2000), though no longer the World's Tallest Wooden Flagpole, Sir Douglas is still standing tall in Toronto.

Also assisting in "Operation Flagpole" were:
Greater Victoria Water Board
Wickheim Timber Shows
Canadian National Railways
Hendrie and Company, Ltd.
Andy Hamilton Crane Service, Ltd.
Ainsworth Electric Company, Ltd.
Heather and Little, Ltd.

Photo Credit: Anonymous

THE PLAQUE

From the Shawnigan Lake region of British Columbia, this Douglas fir flagpole is 184 feet (55.24m) in height,
has a tip diameter of 15 inches (.37m), a butt diameter of 33 inches (.825m), and weighs 35,000 pounds (15,909 kg).
Erected by the Canadian National Exhibition Association.

Congratulations, Sir Douglas Fir!